Slithering Snakes

Sidewinders

by Joanne Mattern

BELLWETHER MEDIA • MINNEAPOLIS, MN

Blastoff! Readers are carefully developed by literacy experts to build reading stamina and move students toward fluency by combining standards-based content with developmentally appropriate text.

Level 1 provides the most support through repetition of high-frequency words, light text, predictable sentence patterns, and strong visual support.

Level 2 offers early readers a bit more challenge through varied sentences, increased text load, and text-supportive special features.

Level 3 advances early-fluent readers toward fluency through increased text load, less reliance on photos, advancing concepts, longer sentences, and more complex special features.

★ **Blastoff! Universe**

Reading Level

Blastoff! Beginners — Grade K

Blastoff! Readers — Grades 1–3

Blastoff! Discovery — Grade 4

This edition first published in 2025 by Bellwether Media, Inc.

Library of Congress Cataloging-in-Publication Data

Names: Mattern, Joanne, 1963- author.
Title: Sidewinders / by Joanne Mattern.
Description: Minneapolis, MN : Bellwether Media, Inc., 2025. | Series: Blastoff! readers: slithering snakes | Includes bibliographical references and index. | Audience: Ages 5-8 | Audience: Grades K-1 | Summary: "Simple text and full-color photography introduce beginning readers to sidewinders. Developed by literacy experts for students in kindergarten through third grade"-- Provided by publisher.
Identifiers: LCCN 2024003103 (print) | LCCN 2024003104 (ebook) | ISBN 9798886870411 (library binding) | ISBN 9781644878859 (ebook)
Subjects: LCSH: Sidewinder (Reptile)--Juvenile literature.
Classification: LCC QL666.O69 M359 2025 (print) | LCC QL666.O69 (ebook) | DDC 597.96--dc23/eng/20240208
LC record available at https://lccn.loc.gov/2024003103
LC ebook record available at https://lccn.loc.gov/2024003104

Editor: Betsy Rathburn Designer: Brittany McIntosh

Printed in the United States of America, North Mankato, MN.

Table of Contents

Horns and Rattles

Sidewinders are rattlesnakes known for their sideways movements.

These **reptiles** live in the southwestern United States. They also live in northwestern Mexico.

Sidewinders are small. They grow about 2 feet (0.6 meters) long.

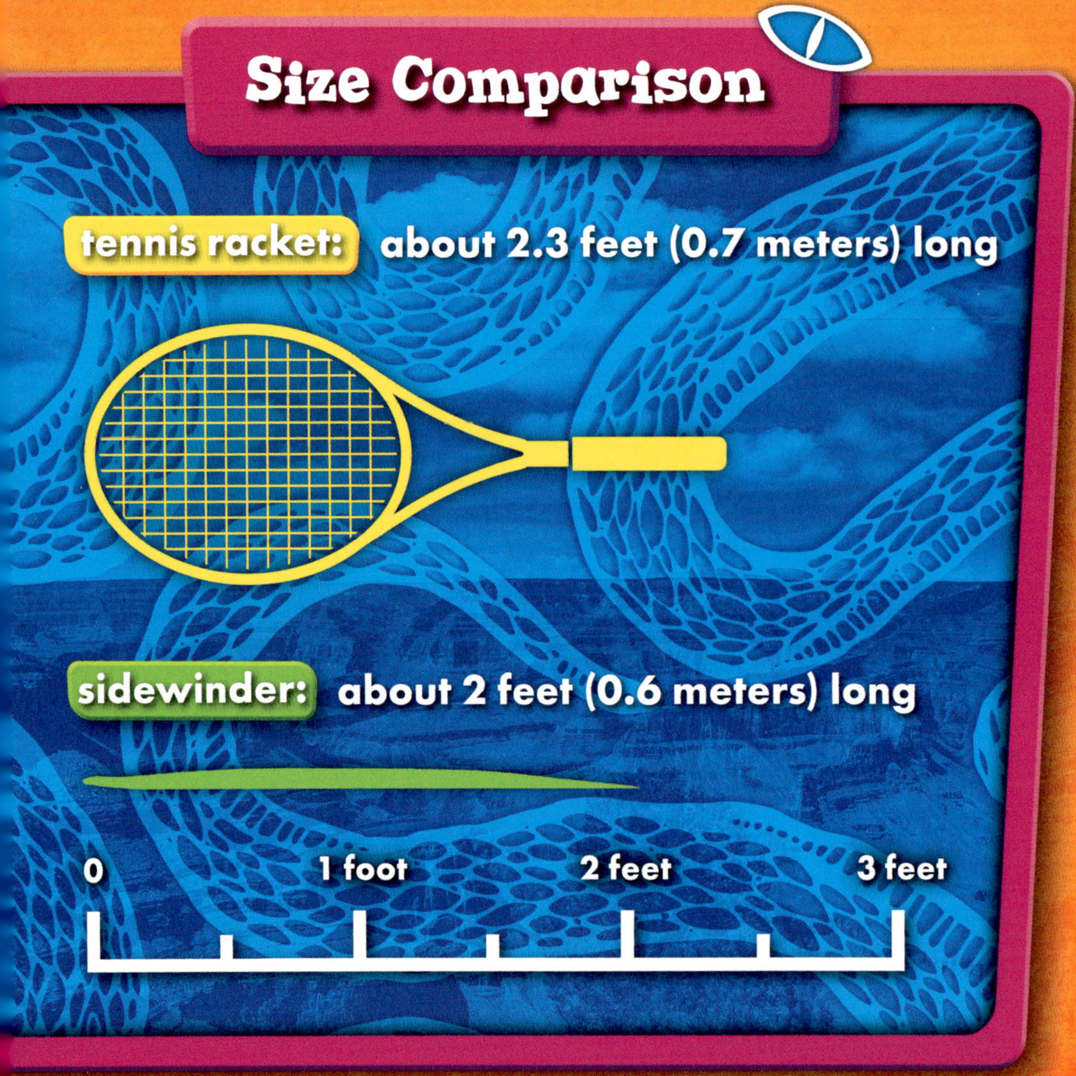

They weigh less than 1 pound (0.5 kilograms).

Sidewinders have tan bodies with dark spots.

Raised **scales** near their eyes look like horns. **Rattles** on their tails make noise.

Spot a Sidewinder!

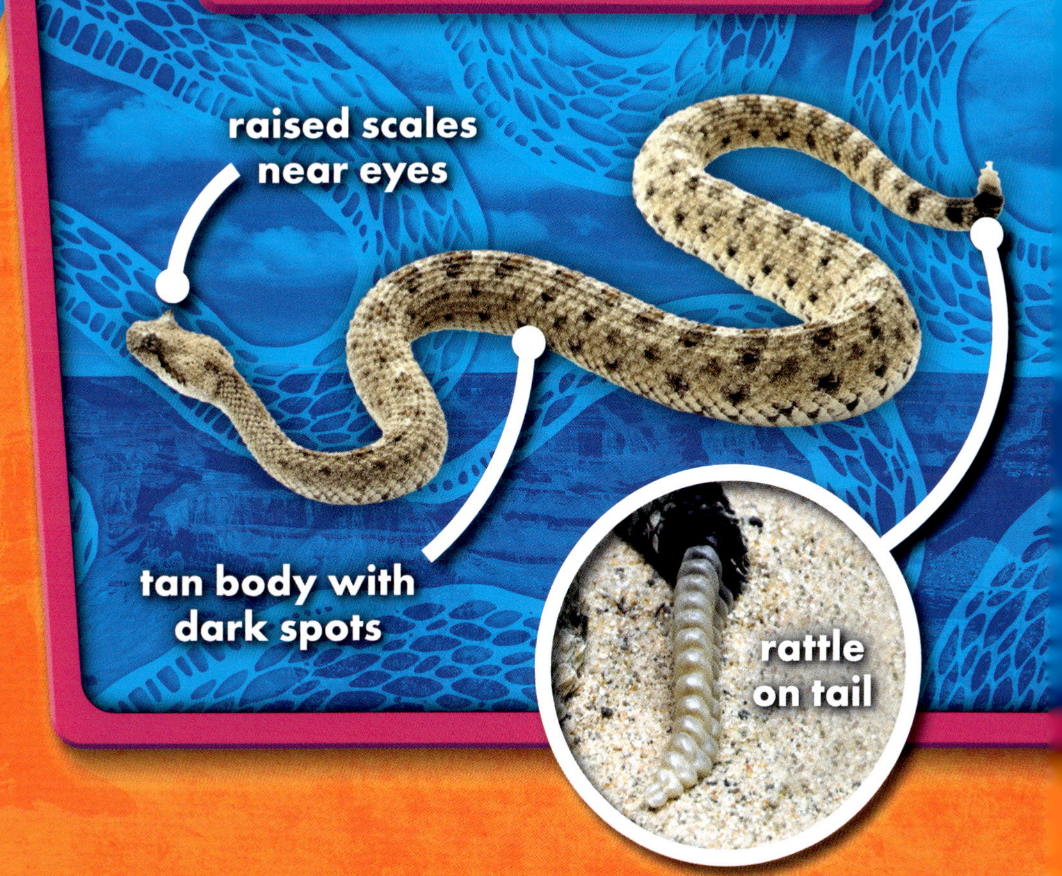

Sand Snakes

Sidewinders live in hot **deserts**. They keep cool in **burrows**.

Sideways movements help them speed across hot sand. They move up to 18 miles (29 kilometers) per hour!

Sidewinders mostly hunt at night. They bury their bodies in sand.

When **prey** comes close, sidewinders bite! Their **venom** takes down lizards, **rodents**, and birds.

Sidewinder Food

Sidewinders are hunted by coyotes, hawks, and king snakes.

Sidewinders shake their rattles to scare **predators** away. They often bite to **defend** themselves!

Sidewinders **hibernate** during the cool winter months. They rest underground.

They come back outside when it is warm again!

Sidewinders Grow Up

Female sidewinders have up to 18 babies at once. The babies are born in burrows.

They go outside after
about one week.

Sidewinders **shed** their skin as they grow. This makes their rattles bigger. In three years, they can have their own babies.

Watch out for speedy sidewinders!

Sidewinder Stats

status in the wild: least concern

life span: up to 20 years

Glossary

burrows—tunnels or holes that some animals use for homes

defend—to keep safe

deserts—dry lands with few plants and little rainfall

hibernate—to pass the winter by sleeping or resting

predators—animals that hunt other animals for food

prey—animals that are hunted by other animals for food

rattles—groups of hard, loose scales that cover the ends of rattlesnake tails

reptiles—cold-blooded animals that have backbones

rodents—small animals that gnaw on their food

shed—to lose fur or skin

scales—plates that cover an animal's body

venom—poison produced by an animal, usually for hunting

To Learn More

AT THE LIBRARY

Davies, Monika. *Deadly Rattlesnakes*. New York, N.Y.: Gareth Stevens Publishing, 2023.

Perish, Patrick. *Sidewinders*. Minneapolis, Minn.: Bellwether Media, 2019.

Wilson, Libby. *Rattlesnakes*. Mendota Heights, Minn.: North Star Editions, 2023.

ON THE WEB

FACTSURFER

Factsurfer.com gives you a safe, fun way to find more information.

1. Go to www.factsurfer.com.
2. Enter "sidewinders" into the search box and click 🔍.
3. Select your book cover to see a list of related content.

Index

The images in this book are reproduced through the courtesy of: Susan M Snyder, front cover, pp. 18, 20; fivespots, pp. 3, 9, 23; Mark_Kostich, p. 4; Creeping Things, p. 7; Rusty Dodson, p. 8; Arterra Picture Library/ Alamy, pp. 9 (inset), 16; Raul Arroyo, p. 10; SuperStock/ Daniel Heuclin/ Biosphoto, pp. 11, 15; Ross Way/ Alamy, p. 12; Rick & Nora Bowers/ Alamy, pp. 12-13; Charles T. Peden, p. 13 (lizards); Sue A Dunning, p. 13 (rodents); David Spates, p. 13 (birds); Marian Murdoch, p. 14; MSMondadori, p. 17; Mark Kostich/ Adobe Stock, p. 19; Nature Picture Library/ Alamy, pp. 20-21.